NUCLEAR
ARMS RACE

© Aladdin Books Ltd

Designed and produced by
Aladdin Books Ltd
70 Old Compton Street
London W1

First published in
Great Britain in 1986 by
Franklin Watts
12a Golden Square
London W1

ISBN 86313 394 0

The author, Nigel Hawkes, is diplomatic correspondent to The Observer
newspaper, London.

The consultant, Dr Philip Towle, is author of East-West Relations and
a Fellow of Queens' College, Cambridge.

The front cover photograph shows a US atmospheric nuclear test.
The back cover photograph shows President Reagan and General
Secretary Gorbachev at the Geneva Summit, 1985.

Contents

Introduction	4
The race begins	6
Strike power	8
A race on many levels	10
The silent war	12
Balance of terror	14
Nuclear deterrence	16
Arms control	18
The widening race	20
Levels of risk	22
Nuclear testing	24
Nuclear protest	26
How can we stop?	28
Hard facts	30
Index	32

NUCLEAR
ARMS RACE

NIGEL HAWKES

Illustrated by
Ron Hayward Associates

Franklin Watts
London : New York : Toronto : Sydney

Introduction

On 6 August 1945 the first nuclear weapon was used to destroy the city of Hiroshima, in Japan. Today there are more than 20,000 nuclear weapons in the world, most of them much more powerful than that first weapon. They are the result of an intense rivalry between the two great powers, the United States and the Soviet Union, each determined not to be dominated by the other. Neither side can use its weapons, for dread of devastating retaliation. Peace is maintained by fear: the fear of the appalling destruction and millions of deaths a nuclear war would bring.

▽ The Hiroshima bomb demolished buildings over an area of ten km² (four sq miles). Only the tattered remnants of the Museum of Science survived. Ruined, it still stands today as a reminder of the terrible power of nuclear weapons.

How has it happened? Both sides fear and mistrust the other, and believe that only by matching the other, weapon for weapon, can the uneasy balance of terror be maintained. Many attempts have been made to dispel the mistrust and reduce the level of weapons by negotiation. The most recent round of talks began in Geneva during 1985, the climax of which was a summit meeting between the two leaders of the superpowers. The Geneva talks followed four decades of similar negotiations aimed at limiting the nuclear arms race. This book is about the race; how it began, what it involves, and how it might be controlled.

5

The race begins

The first nuclear weapons were built in secrecy and in haste during the Second World War. Afraid that the Germans under Adolf Hitler might be first to build a bomb based on the new discovery of nuclear fission – and would use it to win the war in a single blow – an Allied team based at Los Alamos in New Mexico raced to get the weapon first.

By 1945 they had succeeded, but by then Germany was defeated. Instead it was the Americans who used the bomb in the Far East to bring the war against Japan to a rapid conclusion. Faced with the destruction of Hiroshima and Nagasaki, Japan surrendered.

For several years only the Americans had the bomb. But in 1949 the Russians, whose wartime alliance with the US had broken down, tested their first atom bomb. During the 1950s both sides developed bombs of even greater power, based on nuclear fusion – hydrogen bombs.

▷ The mushroom cloud of a nuclear explosion rises high into the atmosphere after a French test at Mururoa Atoll test site in the South Pacific, 1971. The French entered the nuclear arms race in 1960 when they exploded their first test bomb in the Sahara.

The Cold War – A history of mistrust

America and Russia had fought as allies against fascism. But they soon fell out once Germany was beaten. Stalin, the Soviet leader, imposed communist governments in the countries of Eastern Europe. These governments were committed to the ideal of common ownership of industry and property by the people and had to be pro-Soviet. However, the governments were set up despite Stalin's earlier promises to hold free elections in Eastern Europe. Rightly or wrongly, Western leaders saw this move as a plan to spread communism worldwide.

In 1948 Stalin tried to cut off Berlin from the West. By 1950 a war of words – the Cold War – had begun; an arms build-up was under way on both sides.

The Western nations formed an alliance called the North Atlantic Treaty Organisation (NATO) while the Soviet Union and its satellites set up the Warsaw Pact. In 1962 the world came close to war when Russia placed missiles on Cuba, an ally just 144km (90 miles) from the American coast. Attempts to build a better relationship in the 1970s, called "detente", broke down in 1979 when the Soviet Union invaded Afghanistan.

▷ The Titan ballistic missile (right) has a range of 14,960km (9,300 miles) and it can place its huge 9 megaton warhead (the largest in the US armoury) with an accuracy of 900m (3,000 ft). By 1988, all the 54 Titan-II missiles deployed by the US will have been withdrawn: the US is replacing Titan-II with even more accurate missiles, such as the Peacekeeper. (One megaton is the equivalent of one million tonnes of TNT.)

fireball

metal vaporises to gas

metal melts

rubber and plastics ignite, wood burns

third degree burns, charred skin, fabrics ignite

| ground zero | 4.5km (2.8 miles) | 6.2km (3.9 miles) | 13.3km (8.3 miles) |

Strike power

The power of a nuclear explosion is almost unimaginable. The blast will flatten buildings for several kilometres in every direction, while the heat will melt roads and set light to forests. Anybody looking directly at the explosion will be blinded by the flash, even as far as 160km (100 miles) away. The explosion will also produce invisible but deadly radiation, which will cause many to die of radiation sickness. Radioactive dust ("fall-out") from the mushroom cloud will cause others to die months, or even years, later.

Today nuclear weapons can be carried swiftly and accurately to their targets. Intercontinental ballistic missiles, for example the American MX missile (also known as the "Peacekeeper"), travel through space from launch to target and land within 100m (109 yards) of where they were aimed. Because of their accuracy and range, ICBMs are capable of striking deep into the enemy's territory and are a vital part of each superpower's "strategic" nuclear weapon arsenal. Defending cities against attack by hundreds of ICBMs launched at the same time is currently impossible.

▽ About half the energy from a nuclear explosion is released as heat: the rest as blast and radiation. Close to the centre of the explosion, the temperature is near to that of the surface of the Sun, whose energy is produced by the same nuclear fusion reactions. If the weapon is exploded in the air rather than on the ground, the tremendous heat produced can spread outwards and cause injury and damage as far as 40km (25 miles) away. The diagram shows the effects of heat, spreading out from the site of explosion.

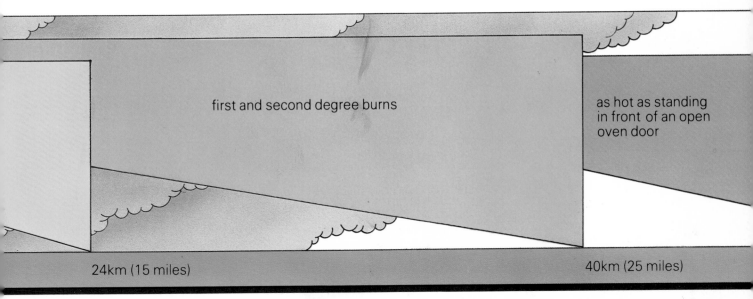

first and second degree burns

as hot as standing in front of an open oven door

24km (15 miles)

40km (25 miles)

A race on many levels

▽ The most powerful land-based missiles are fired from deep concrete silos, tough enough to protect them from anything less than a direct hit by an enemy warhead.

There is not one arms race, but many. The superpowers now have every type of nuclear weapon imaginable: bombs, missiles with ranges from 160 to 12,800km (100 to 8,000 miles), artillery shells, mines, even nuclear depth charges for attacking submarines. Some missiles are based in deep concrete bunkers, called "silos", for protection. Others (like the Soviet SS-20) are mounted on mobile launchers to make detection harder. The American cruise missiles, also mobile, are like unmanned aircraft, flying close to the ground to escape detection.

Soviet SS-19
ICBM

The American B-52 Stratofortress bomber which carries short-range attack missiles

missile silo

The total number of ICBMs is limited by a treaty – but not the total number of warheads. So to increase striking power, each ICBM has been given many warheads, each of which is aimed at a separate target.

They are called MIRVs – for Multiple Independently-targeted Re-entry Vehicles. MIRVs threaten the delicate nuclear balance between the superpowers because they might make it possible for one side to launch a surprise attack and destroy all the other side's silo-based missiles in a single "first strike".

▽ Missiles such as the Soviet SS-19 may carry up to six warheads, which separate from the "bus" carrying them high in the atmosphere, then fall on widely-spaced targets on enemy territory.

missile bus

warheads

Ballistic missiles are remarkable pieces of engineering. They weigh between 10 and 200 tonnes (depending on their range) yet can accelerate to a speed of almost 2,900km (1,800 miles) an hour in just five minutes from a standing start. If they are to impact within three-quarters of a kilometre (half a mile) of their target, their speed must be just right to within one part in a thousand. Missiles are more effective, and far more frightening, than bombs dropped from aircraft. They fly quicker, are just as accurate, and much harder to stop. But they have one big drawback: once launched, they cannot be recalled.

Intercontinental ballistic missile (ICBM): range over 5,000km (3,100 miles)

Intermediate-range ballistic missile (IRBM): range 200 to 5,000km (124 to 3,100 miles)

strategic bomber: combat range over 3,000km (1,850 miles)

Short-range ballistic missile (SRBM): range up to 200km (124 miles)

The silent war

The danger of a first strike against land-based missiles sent the nuclear arms race under the oceans. Submarines armed with nuclear missiles and driven by nuclear reactors can patrol undetected for three months at a time, always ready to strike at the enemy homeland if war breaks out.

The first nuclear submarines stabilised the nuclear balance. Their missiles were too inaccurate for a first strike, but their invulnerability meant they were always available to retaliate against enemy cities in a "second strike" – a powerful deterrent against attack.

American "Benjamin Franklin" class submarines like the *USS Will Rogers* (above) carry Trident C-4 missiles fired from missile tubes. Open missile tubes can be seen left on the *USS Ohio* of the "Ohio" class.

A single Polaris submarine, with 16 missiles, packs as much explosive power as was used in bombing in the whole of the Second World War. For the moment, submarines remain very difficult to detect. However, developments in electronics, for example the use of sensors scattered on the sea bed, could increase the likelihood of submarine detection and consequent destruction. Such advances would risk unbalancing the nuclear equation because one country could destroy the other's second strike potential.

Balance of terror

Both the US and the USSR today have far more nuclear weapons than they really need to deter attack. The arms race has careered out of control as each has striven to keep up with the other.

US forces are divided between land-based, submarine-based and bomber-based nuclear weapons. The main land-based missile is the Minuteman, which dates from the 1960s. The long-range strategic bomber, the B-52, is even older, having been in service since the mid-1950s. The heart of the American strategic forces is the large fleet of nuclear submarines. The US also has shorter-range cruise and Pershing-2 missiles in Europe.

The American arsenal consists of a "triad" of land, sea and air-based nuclear weapons. In fact, the US actually has fewer nuclear missile submarines than the USSR (35 against 77) and they carry less missiles (592 against 946). However, on a warhead count the US is ahead, as the chart shows. Both sides have a similar number of nuclear-capable aircraft (297 US, 303 USSR), but the US aircraft are more heavily armed with bombs, air-to-surface missiles and air-launched cruise missiles. The US has intermediate-range and cruise missiles in Europe but far fewer than the USSR.

ICBM warheads (Intercontinental ballistic missiles) – 2,130

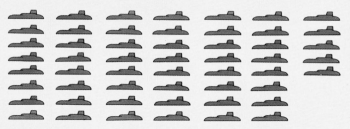

SLBM warheads (Sea-launched ballistic missiles) – 5,344

ASM warheads (Air-to-surface missiles), ALCM warheads (Air-launched cruise missiles) and nuclear bombs – 3,296

IRBM warheads (Intermediate-range ballistic missiles) and cruise warheads – 102

The most important Soviet missiles are the big land-based SS-18s and SS-19s. The SS-18 is the world's biggest missile and can carry ten MIRVed warheads, each 25 times as powerful as the bomb which destroyed Hiroshima. The USSR has fewer bombers but more submarine-based missiles than the US. However, because of the policy of placing many warheads on each missile, the US still has more strike power at sea.

During the 1970s, the USSR deployed a new intermediate-range system, the SS-20, designed to hit targets in Europe. It was to counter the threat of the SS-20s that NATO agreed in 1979 to deploy cruise and Pershing-2 missiles in Europe.

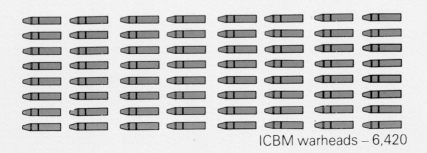

ICBM warheads – 6,420

SLBM warheads – 2,122

Since the development of Mirvs, it is the number of warheads, not missiles, which matters. The chart shows the warhead balance in 1984.

ASM and ALCM warheads and nuclear bombs – 1,052

The Soviet Union's greatest strength is its land-based missile force. It outnumbers the US both in missiles (1,398 against 1,030) and, overwhelmingly, in warheads. This is because its missiles are much more heavily MIRVed than the American land-based Minuteman. The USSR has also concentrated on intermediate-range missiles based in Europe. Each of the SS-20s carries three warheads, and more than 400 have been deployed. In addition, the USSR has 810 launchers of shorter-range missiles (not counted here) against 78 US Pershing-1 launchers based in Europe.

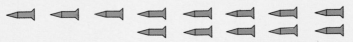

IRBM warheads – 1,320

source: US – Soviet Military Balance 1980-1985, Brassey's

Nuclear deterrence

▽ Sophisticated radars, like the huge white domes at Fylingdales, UK, are vital to nuclear deterrence. Together with satellites, they would provide early warning of attack, enabling a retaliatory strike to be launched in time. It is the certainty of such retaliation that deters attack, and forms the basis of the concept of deterrence.

The appalling consequences of a nuclear war have changed the way people think. Nobody could win such a war, because some missiles would survive a first-strike attack to wreak a terrible revenge. This knowledge deters both sides, creating an uneasy peace based on the certainty that both sides would be destroyed in a war – the concept known to nuclear strategists as mutually assured destruction (MAD).

To maintain deterrence, each new weapon developed by one side must be matched by the other, in a spiral of escalation. Nuclear deterrence is frightening: but it has helped prevent world war for more than 40 years.

Can nuclear deterrence ever be replaced? President Reagan believes so, and has launched a 26,000 million dollar research project to find out. It is called the Strategic Defence Initiative (or "Star Wars") programme and its aim is to produce a missile-proof defence based on advanced technology. The US claims that Star Wars will scrap offensive nuclear weapons because it would provide such an effective shield against attack.

Many people doubt that Star Wars will work, or suspect that it will be so "leaky" that all the Soviet Union needs to do is to build a few more missiles to overwhelm it.

▽ The "Star Wars" system would attack missiles at different stages in their flight. A satellite tracks the missile launch (1). Laser attack by the first layer (2). Second layer attack (3) is aimed at the missile "bus" which carries the warheads. A tracking satellite (4) sends information about surviving warheads to another laser (5). An infrared probe (6) is sent into space and passes information about remaining warheads to (7) which attacks these with non-nuclear devices launched from Earth.

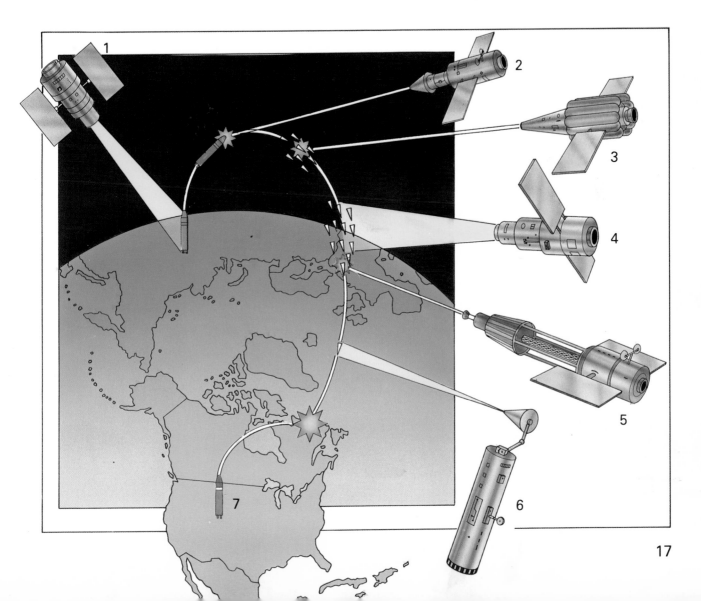

Arms control

Conscious of the dangers and costs of the arms race, both sides have tried to bring it under control by negotiation. They have largely failed. Why?

The principal reason is the same as that which caused the arms race in the first place – mutual mistrust. While there is no trust, there can be no concessions; so both sides have used arms control talks to try to gain advantages over the other. The advantages have usually turned out to be illusory. Only when both sides' interests were identical has real progress been made – in stopping atmospheric testing and limiting anti-missile systems. Difficulties over verification have also hindered progress.

Talks to date

1963 Hotline Agreement: after the Cuban missile crisis, both sides agreed to establish a direct link – the hotline – to control future crises.

1963 Partial Test Ban Treaty, banning nuclear tests in the atmosphere, was signed by the US, USSR, and UK. The aim was to control radioactive pollution: tests moved underground.

1967 Outer Space Treaty banned the placing of nuclear weapons in space or on the Moon.

1968 Non-Proliferation Treaty was designed to control the spread of nuclear weapons. So far it has worked fairly well.

The first important nuclear arms control treaty – the treaty banning nuclear tests in the atmosphere – was signed by President John F. Kennedy (right) and General Secretary Nikita Khruschev (above) on 5 August 1963. It did not stop testing, but it did reduce the poisoning of the air by fall-out.

Two agreements limiting strategic weapons have been signed. In SALT-1 (Strategic Arms Limitation Talks) President Richard Nixon and General Secretary Leonid Brezhnev set ceilings on the number of missiles each could have. However, at American insistence, no limits were set on the improvement, by MIRVing, of those missiles. This was a mistake – the Soviet rockets were more powerful and could take more MIRVed warheads than the American ones.

SALT-2, signed by President Jimmy Carter and Brezhnev, set new limits. But the treaty was never ratified as it was withdrawn from the US Senate after the Soviet invasion of Afghanistan.

1971 Sea-bed Treaty banned the placing of nuclear weapons on the sea bed.

1972 SALT-1, set limits on the numbers of US and Soviet land and sea-based missiles.

1972 Anti-Ballistic Missile Treaty, part of SALT-1, limited the deployment of systems designed to defend against missiles. A successful treaty now endangered by the American "Star Wars" programme.

1974 Threshold Agreement set a limit of 150 kilotonnes (thousands of tonnes of TNT) for underground explosions.

1979 SALT-2 set new, but high, limits on strategic systems.

President Richard M. Nixon (right) and General Secretary Leonid Brezhnev (above) negotiated several agreements during the years of "detente". The SALT-1 and Anti-Ballistic Missile treaties were both landmarks showing that agreement between the two superpowers is possible.

The widening race

Alongside the race between the superpowers, a second and equally dangerous arms race has been going on. Britain was the first to enter when it tested its own bomb in 1952. France joined in, then China and finally, in 1974, India tested a bomb. For the moment, these six are the only known nuclear powers.

Nobody doubts, however, that Israel has a bomb and would use it if her existence was threatened. South Africa, too, certainly has the capacity to make a bomb and may already have done so. Pakistan is also rumoured to be close to testing its first bomb.

The sinister spread of nuclear knowledge has been slowed down by the Nuclear Non-Proliferation Treaty of 1968, under which more than 120 countries have promised not to build bombs. In return, the nuclear countries party to the treaty (USA, USSR and UK) have agreed to help non-nuclear states to develop nuclear energy for peaceful use.

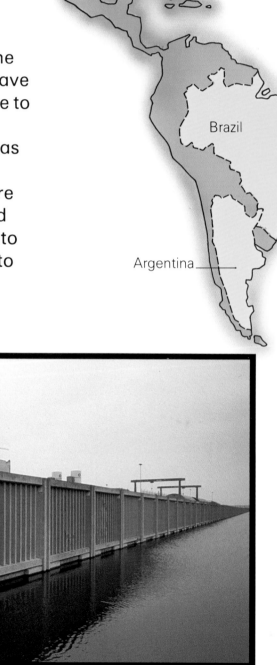

USA

Cuba

Brazil

Argentina

The well protected nuclear power plant at Kalkar, West Germany

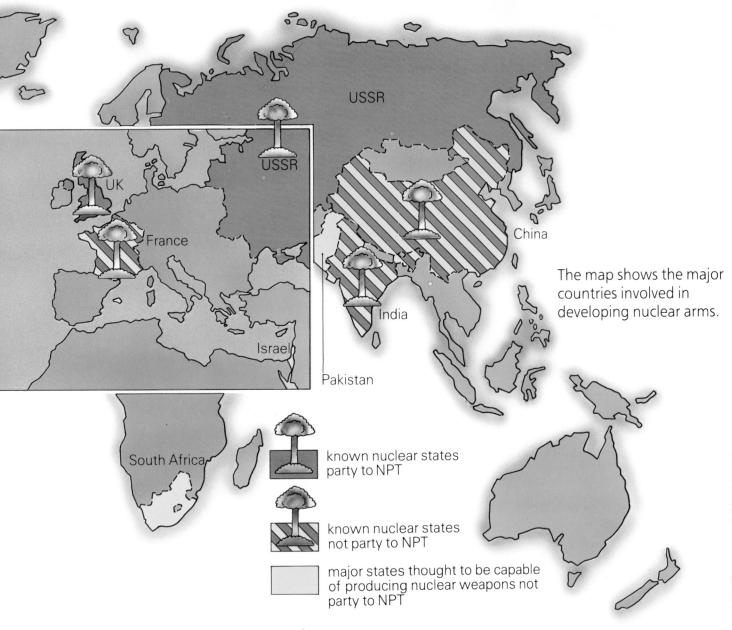

USSR

USSR

UK

France

Israel

Pakistan

China

India

The map shows the major countries involved in developing nuclear arms.

South Africa

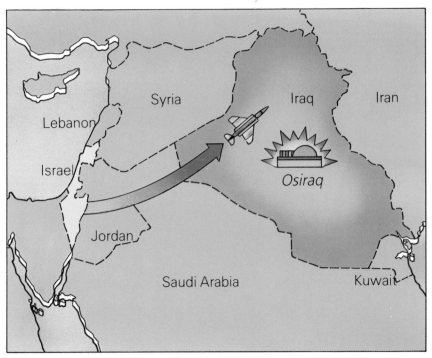

known nuclear states party to NPT

known nuclear states not party to NPT

major states thought to be capable of producing nuclear weapons not party to NPT

Lebanon

Syria

Iraq

Iran

Israel

Osiraq

Jordan

Saudi Arabia

Kuwait

◁ Even the simplest and smallest of nuclear reactors can be used to provide the raw material for an atomic bomb. In June 1981 Israel became convinced that Iraq was using a research reactor it had bought from France to produce a bomb. Although Iraq had both signed and ratified the NPT, Israel did not accept that its intentions were peaceful – the Israelis were afraid that the Iraqis were manufacturing a bomb which might be used against them in all out war. In a daring air raid on 7 June, Israel destroyed the Osiraq reactor.

Levels of risk

◁ The American Lance missile is a battlefield weapon which can be fitted with nuclear warheads. It is designed as a mobile battlefield support missile and has a range of 110km (68 miles) for use in a "limited" nuclear war against specific targets. Lance missiles are deployed in Europe to counter the threat of the Soviet SS-21 but they could not be used *en masse* without destroying West Germany in the process. The photograph also illustrates the clothing worn by soldiers to protect them from radiation.

Neither side wants a nuclear war, or intends deliberately to start one. But might the world stumble into disaster by accident? The greatest danger lies along the border between East and West in Europe, where NATO faces the Warsaw Pact. Each side is racing against the other not only to develop sophisticated conventional weapons, but also tactical and battlefield nuclear weapons – mines, artillery shells, short-range missiles and nuclear-capable aircraft. Many of these weapons, though described as "tactical", have warheads several times as powerful as the Hiroshima bomb.

Are so many nuclear weapons necessary? NATO has recently withdrawn some, but its fundamental problem remains: it is outnumbered at least two to one by Warsaw Pact conventional forces. To fend off invasion, it could need to use battlefield nuclear weapons – thus risking escalation to a full-scale nuclear exchange with devastating consequences.

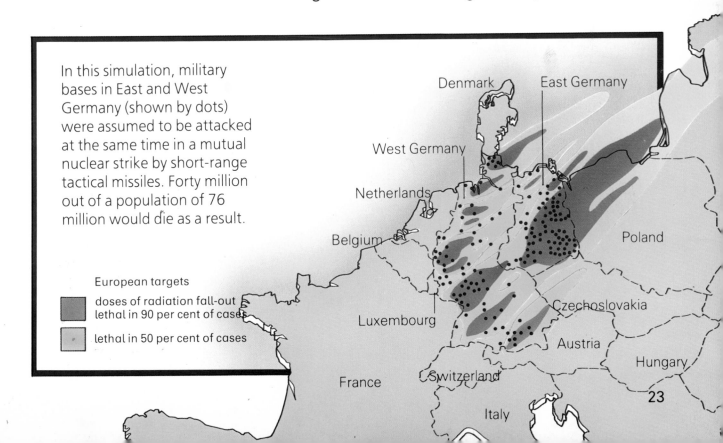

In this simulation, military bases in East and West Germany (shown by dots) were assumed to be attacked at the same time in a mutual nuclear strike by short-range tactical missiles. Forty million out of a population of 76 million would die as a result.

European targets

◾ doses of radiation fall-out lethal in 90 per cent of cases

▫ lethal in 50 per cent of cases

Denmark   East Germany

West Germany

Netherlands

Belgium   Poland

Luxembourg   Czechoslovakia

Austria

France   Switzerland   Hungary

Italy

Nuclear testing

The first nuclear weapons were tested in the atmosphere, producing the familiar mushroom cloud. But since the Partial Test Ban treaty of 1963, testing by the UK, the US and the USSR has been carried out in caverns underground, where it can cause no pollution to the atmosphere.

Without tests, it would be impossible to develop new weapons. So a complete ban on testing, if it could be agreed and enforced, would eventually control the nuclear arms race. Negotiations in the late 1970s made some progress, but were abandoned in 1980 when the US pulled out. One problem was verification – checking whether either side was cheating.

Today scientists have developed such sensitive instruments that they believe secret tests could be detected. So a ban could be enforced, if both sides agreed.

▽ During the 1950s, Britain carried out a series of nuclear tests in the Australian bush. As a result kilometres of land became contaminated by radioactive fall-out. This meant that many Aborigines had to leave their traditional homelands and settle elsewhere. Today they wish to return and are demonstrating for this right – as this television news-shot shows.

The Greenpeace ship *Rainbow Warrior* protesting against French nuclear testing

▷ Atmospheric nuclear tests send a dirty smear of radioactivity spreading around the world, carried by the winds high in the atmosphere. Within a week of this 1966 test by China, the fall-out had been detected in a ring around the Northern Hemisphere.

11 May 10 May

USSR

China
9 May

12 May

17 May

USA

13 May

15 May

14 May

Nuclear protest

 The Campaign for Nuclear Disarmament (CND) originated the famous peace symbol now seen all over the world. CND argues that nuclear weapons are immoral, and could never be used because of the millions who would die.

Greenpeace is an environmental group which runs many campaigns. It argues that all types of nuclear testing should be banned. It claims that several atolls in the Pacific have been destroyed by underground testing and are in danger of collapse.

The anti-nuclear arguments have been taken up all over Europe by political parties. In Britain the Labour Party is committed to the removal of American bases from British soil, while the Conservatives believe that Britain should not only retain nuclear weapons but improve them by buying Trident submarines. In France and Germany the "Green" parties, which favour environmental causes, have argued strongly against nuclear weapons. But there are no open anti-nuclear protesters in the Soviet Union – the only protest allowed there is against American weapons.

The failure of governments to control nuclear weapons has brought thousands of people out on to the streets. Huge demonstrations in western countries have shown how strongly they feel about the threat of nuclear war. People in the Soviet Union no doubt feel just as strongly – but there public protests against government policy are forbidden.

The Campaign for Nuclear Disarmament (CND), active since the 1950s, argues that Britain should give up its nuclear weapons, on its own, to set a moral example to the rest.

Some anti-nuclear protesters are pacifists — they oppose war of any sort. Others argue that defending yourself with conventional weapons is permissible, but that nuclear weapons are immoral and nuclear deterrence unstable. Countries that invest so much in weapons will eventually use them, they say.

Other groups concentrate on trying to persuade their governments to reach arms control agreements. The Freeze movement wants an immediate ban on development, testing and deployment of new weapons.

▽ The Freeze movement, launched in the US in the early 1980s, gained considerable support and its policies were adopted by the defeated Democratic candidate in the 1984 election, Walter Mondale. It campaigns for an immediate freeze, by both sides, on the development, testing and deployment of new nuclear weapons, as a prelude to nuclear disarmament.

How can we stop?

Will the arms race ever end? The record of discussions on arms restrictions has been, to date, disappointing. But the central issue remains: the presence on Earth of sufficient nuclear weapons to destroy everything on it three times over, whilst the stockpile of weapons continues to grow. Often proposals from one side tend to twist the race towards a new balance of terror and breed fresh suspicion. Star Wars, claimed by the US as a defence system, is feared by the USSR for its "first-strike" potential.

Consequently, the USSR continues to develop its own advanced technology defence weapons. It is thought that these include weapons for attacking satellites and missiles based in space.

▽ Politicians have compared the nuclear armoury of both sides but since the make-up of the two systems is so different, different balances can be drawn up. In the meantime, escalation continues.

Nevertheless, discussions between the superpowers remain our only hope and some agreements have been reached and upheld. For example, The Anti-Ballistic Missile Treaty of 1972 limiting the spread of defensive missiles, is still being adhered to. Moreover, when President Reagan met General Secretary Gorbachev in Geneva late in 1985, both agreed that strategic weapons ought to be reduced by half.

"Nations do not distrust each other because they are armed" Reagan told Gorbachev. "They are armed because they distrust each other." Only if further meetings dispel that mistrust can there be serious hopes of limiting the nuclear arms race and ending the balance of terror.

▽ In November 1985 President Ronald Reagan met General Secretary Mikhail Gorbachev in Geneva — the first top level meeting between the two countries' leaders for six years. They made some progress, and agreed to meet again — but signed no arms control agreements.

Hard facts

Argentina
A potential nuclear power which has not signed the NPT, Argentina has nuclear power stations and, according to some reports, a small-scale plant for producing weapon-grade uranium. But the election of a democratic government in 1983 may have slowed down the nuclear weapon programme.

Brazil
A close neighbour and rival of Argentina, Brazil is also thought to have nuclear ambitions! Like its neighbour a non-signatory of the NPT, Brazil and Argentina have signed the Treaty of Tlatelolco, which bans nuclear weapons from Latin America. Restored democracy may dampen nuclear ambitions.

Britain
First nuclear test 1952. Heart of nuclear strike force is four Polaris submarines, carrying 64 missiles, each with three warheads. Britain also has aircraft capable of carrying nuclear weapons (Jaguar and Tornado) and a range of tactical nuclear weapons on the European front.

China
First nuclear test 1964. China has deployed four missiles, one of which, the CSS-4, has full ICBM range, primarily designed to deter attack from the Soviet Union.

France
First nuclear test 1960. France has 18 IRBMs with a 3,218 km (2,000 miles) range, and six submarines each carrying 16 missiles, with a single 1 megaton warhead. France also has nuclear-capable aircraft, and the short-range Pluton tactical missile, launched from a mobile platform.

India
First nuclear test 1974. Since then, no further tests, and regular denials from the Indian Government that it has produced any nuclear weapons. It can probably be assumed that India does have a few bombs, however, and the aircraft to deliver them. India's test was a direct response to China's.

Israel
Although there has never been an Israeli nuclear test, few doubt that Israel has the material and the ability to build a bomb. Most analysts assume that this weapon – or several weapons – is ready for rapid assembly and use if Israel were ever threatened with military defeat.

Libya
Libya probably lacks either the knowledge or the materials for nuclear weapons, but its friendship with Pakistan and the erratic behaviour of its leader Colonel Gadafy, have caused anxieties.

New Zealand
At the opposite extreme, New Zealand has declared itself a nuclear-free zone. It will not permit visits from ships carrying nuclear weapons, and has made it an offence for any New Zealander to try to develop such weapons. This policy has brought it into conflict with the US.

Pakistan
Following the Indian lead, Pakistan by 1985 was believed to be very close to testing its first nuclear weapon. It would be the first Muslim country to have a nuclear weapon, and the danger might be that it would transfer the technology to other Islamic countries, including Libya.

South Africa
Most analysts believe that South Africa has the technology to divert nuclear material from power stations to make nuclear weapons. As South Africa has not signed the NPT, her nuclear activities are not officially known or restricted.

Taiwan
The last refuge of the nationalist Chinese defeated by the Communists in 1949, Taiwan is a possible nuclear power. The rationale would be to defend itself against the People's Republic of China. If Taiwan is working towards a bomb, it might succeed by 1990.

Chronology

1939 Otto Hahn and Lise Meitner, working in Berlin, discover that atoms of uranium will split in two, releasing huge amounts of energy.

1945 At dawn on 16 July, in the deserts of New Mexico, the discovery is turned into a weapon as the first atomic bomb is tested.

1945 The first two production bombs, one made from uranium and the second from plutonium, are dropped on Japan. Hiroshima and Nagasaki are destroyed, and Japan surrenders.

1949 The American monopoly of the atom bomb is broken as the Soviet Union tests its first bomb. The US presses on to develop even more powerful and deadly weapons based on nuclear fusion.

1954 America tests the first practical hydrogen bomb, with a 15 megaton yield.

1955 The Soviet Union tests its first H-bomb, with a 1.6 megaton yield.

1957 The Soviet Union puts the first satellite, Sputnik-1, into Earth's orbit, and tests the SS-6 ICBM.

1962 Cuban missile crisis: Soviet leader Khruschev withdraws Soviet missiles and bombers from Cuba after the US threatens to search all Soviet ships in the area.

1972 SALT-1 agreement begins period of reduced tension known as "detente". But Soviet Union continues arms build-up at undiminished speed.

1979 Soviet invasion of Afghanistan finally ends detente.

1985 US and USSR resume arms control negotiations.

Glossary

Ballistic: a missile which moves under gravity after initial powered and guided stage.

Cold War: period of high tension beginning in the late 1940s; intense mutual distrust expressed in words rather than fighting.

First-strike: used (correctly) to describe an attack which destroys all enemy weapons before they can be used and (incorrectly) to describe missiles for use against military targets.

Fission: the splitting of the atom of uranium or plutonium in the atom bomb.

Fusion: the combining together of light atoms of hydrogen to release energy in the hydrogen bomb.

IRBM: Intermediate-range ballistic missile, i.e. SS-20, Pershing-2.

MIRVs: Multiple Independently-targeted Re-entry Vehicles. The practice of placing up to 10-15 warheads, each with its own target, on a single missile. Each re-entry vehicle is computer-guided.

Radiation: damaging rays and particles emitted by nuclear fission and fusion. Includes X-rays and gamma-rays.

SALT: Strategic Arms Limitation Talks.

SDI: Strategic Defence Initiative American research programme (Star Wars) to investigate defence against ballistic missiles.

Strategic: used to describe long-range nuclear weapons capable of striking into the heart of enemy territory.

Tactical: used to describe short-range nuclear weapons for battlefield warfare.

Verification: system for ensuring that both sides adhere to treaties, perhaps including on-site inspections.

Index

A Afghanistan, 6, 31
Argentina, 30

B bombs, see weapons
Brazil, 30
Britain, 20-21, 26, 30

C China, 20-21
CND, 26
Cold War, 6
cruise missiles, see
weapons: missiles
Cuba, 6, 18, 31

D "detente", 6, 19, 31
deterrence, 12, 14, 16-
17, 27
disarmament, 26-27

F fall-out, 9, 24, 25, 31
France, 20-21, 26, 30
Freeze movement, 27

G Germany, 20, 23, 26
Greenpeace, 26

H Hiroshima, 4, 6, 15, 23,
31

I India, 20-21, 30
Israel, 20-21, 30

J Japan, 4, 6, 31

L Libya, 30

M missiles, see weapons

N Nagasaki, 6, 31
NATO, 6, 15, 23
New Zealand, 30

P Pakistan, 20-21, 30
Pershing-2, see weapons:
missiles
Polaris, see weapons:
submarines

R radioactivity, 18, 23, 24-
25
reactors, 13, 21

S SALT talks, 19, 24
satellites, 16-17, 31
South Africa, 20-21, 30
Soviet Union, 4-6, 14-15,
17-19, 21, 26, 28, 31

"Star Wars", 17, 19, 28
submarines, see weapons

T talks, 5, 19, 24, 29, 31
tests, 6, 18, 20, 24-27, 30
treaties, 11, 18-20, 24, 29
Trident, see weapons:
submarines

U United States, 4-6, 14, 15,
17-19, 24, 28, 30-31

W Warsaw Pact, 6, 23
weapons
bombs, 4, 6, 10-11, 14-
15, 20-21, 30, 31
ICBMs, 9, 11, 14-15,
30, 31
MIRVs, 11, 15, 19, 31
missiles, 8-17, 19, 23,
29, 30, 31
range, 9, 11, 15
strike power, 9, 11-13,
15, 16, 23, 28
submarines, 10, 12-15,
28
warheads, 11, 14-15,
17, 19, 31

Photographic Credits:
Cover and pages 22 and 24; Frank Spooner:
pages 4/5; UPI/Bettman: page 7; Associated
Press: pages 8, 10 and 12 (inset); MARS: pages
12/13; Robert Hunt: page 16; MoD: page 18
(left); Rex Features: pages 18 (right), 19 (both)
and 28; Colorific: page 20; Stern: page 24;
Visnews: pages 26/27 and back cover; John
Hillelson: page 29; Washington Post Writer's
Group.

With many thanks to:
Campaign for Nuclear Disarmament
Greenpeace
Ministry of Defence